Jesus
is for You Jesus is for Life

An exploration of the Christian Faith
through drama, for young people

Ray Jackson

First published in 1998 by
KEVIN MAYHEW LTD
Rattlesden
Bury St Edmunds
Suffolk IP30 0SZ

© 1998 Ray Jackson and Sharon Jackson

The right of Ray Jackson and Sharon Jackson to be identified as the authors of this work has been asserted by them in accordance with the Copyright, Designs and Patents Act 1988.

All rights reserved. No part of this publication may be reproduced, stored in a retrieval system, or transmitted, in any form or by any means, electronic, mechanical, photocopying, recording or otherwise, without the prior written permission of the publisher.

0 1 2 3 4 5 6 7 8 9

ISBN 1 84003 195 6
Catalogue No 1500206

Cover illustration: Alan Bedding
Cover design by Jaquetta Sergeant
Typesetting by Louise Selfe
Edited by David Gatward
Printed and bound in Great Britain

Contents

Acknowledgements	5
Introduction	7
Chapter 1: Think BIG *Did Jesus really rise from the dead?*	9
Chapter 2: Stranger than fiction *Who was Jesus?*	18
Chapter 3: Think small *Why did Jesus come to earth?*	26
Chapter 4: Idiot-proof! *Why did Jesus have to die for us?*	33
Chapter 5: Who loves ya, baby? *Did Jesus really die for me?*	39
Chapter 6: The chosen few *How do we become disciples?*	46
Chapter 7: The town drunk *What does Jesus ask from us?*	52
Chapter 8: The gift *What does it mean, to love our neighbour?*	59
Chapter 9: Surprise, surprise! *What was written concerning Jesus?*	66
Chapter 10: Truly amazing! *What does it mean, to live by faith?*	72

BY RAY JACKSON

TAKE 10
TAKE 10 MORE
JESUS IS FOR LIFE

BY SHARON JACKSON

ROLLERCOASTER
SWINGS AND ROUNDABOUTS

About the Authors

Ray Jackson was born in 1951 and *still* doesn't have all the answers! He met his wife at school (and that's not *strictly* correct, since they weren't even married at the time) and went on to become a chartered civil engineer.

He first became involved in Christian youth work around 1989 and has never really fully recovered. He and his wife now lead the youth group 'Stage II', regularly writing and organising productions of drama and music and irregularly taking parties of young people abroad (and similar fits of madness).

Ray started writing books as a young child, something for which he discovered he has a natural gift. Unfortunately, he had turned forty-six before he managed to finish a book, something for which he is *not* naturally gifted.

He and his wife have now settled in North Lincolnshire where they run their property empire, manage their sheep ranch, and live in a world of make-believe. Ray has an incredible memory and can remember the names of every one of his four sheep, though he sometimes forgets one, usually the one with curly horns, you know, what's-its-name?

Sharon Jackson was born in 1975 and grew up on her dad's sheep ranch, although she was allowed in the house occasionally. Her first book, *Rollercoaster*, was published in 1997 after she graduated with a degree in Sociology and Business Management. She now works (at last) and collects hamsters.

For Philip Kennedy.

My brother, not by chance,
but by choice.

Introduction

Does much of the Christian faith seem dry and boring? Do you see Christians as straight-laced kill-joys? This is not how it should be! If Jesus truly is alive and active in the world, then living as one of his followers should be an exciting adventure! In fact, Jesus himself said, 'I have come that you may have life, and have it to the full' (John 10:10b).

Being a disciple is not about looking for the safe, comfortable way through life: Jesus didn't choose that lifestyle and anyone who does is unlikely to achieve very much. Being a disciple is about sticking your neck out and taking risks; and why not? With the King of the Universe on your side, what do you have to lose?

So I want to tell you about the King of the Universe. I must say, I feel woefully inadequate for such a task, but then, who wouldn't? After all, he created everything as far as the telescope, and the microscope, can see (and beyond), whereas I'm just a nobody. But I'm so excited about him and about what he's done for us, and about what he's *doing* for us, that I decided to try anyway!

In effect, this book is a Bible study course, and I know that many people will groan in dismay at this revelation. But how can we hope to learn about God if we don't look at the very book he arranged to be written about himself?

So I hope this is a Bible study course with a difference, a Bible study course with constant reminders of how wonderful our God *really* is! To this end, I've included some astounding truths about the universe God created, and some very human stories about the world in which we live. I just hope these help to reveal some amazing truths about God himself.

The Bible study notes in this book were originally written for my youth resource book, *Jesus is for Life*. This subsequent book, *Jesus is for You*, is more personal and, therefore, more appropriate for an individual. I hope you enjoy reading it. More importantly, I hope you experience some of the awe, the wonder, the reverence and the adoration of which the King of the Universe is indeed worthy.

God bless,

Ray Jackson

Chapter 1
Think BIG

Introduction

Our universe is very old, in fact, around 15,000 million years old! The modern scientific view is that it appeared suddenly, in a single instant, with space, time and matter being created all at once in an enormous Big Bang.

And what a big bang that must have been!

Our sun came into existence much later than this, contracting from an enormous cloud of gas and heating up in the process. When the core temperature rose sufficiently for nuclear fusion to begin, the contraction ceased and the sun became the source of warmth and light that we now see. That was 4,500 million years ago.

The sun is an enormous thermonuclear reactor. Deep within its core, nuclei of hydrogen combine together to form nuclei of helium. In the process, a little energy is released and a little mass (or weight) is lost. The energy released is what powers the sun, heats the solar system, and sustains life on earth. It is equivalent to the energy which would be released if 100,000 million, one megaton hydrogen bombs were detonated every second!

The mass lost per nucleus of helium formed is infinitesimally small but, for the sun as a whole, it amounts to an amazing four million tonnes a second! What is even more amazing is that the sun has been losing four million tonnes a second for the last 4,500 million years, and will continue to do so for a further 4,500 million years, before there is any noticeable change!

We could be forgiven for thinking our sun is

very special, but that isn't the case, in fact, it's quite ordinary. Scientists estimate that our own galaxy, sometimes referred to as the Milky Way, contains something like 15,000 million suns (stars), some of which are thousands of times more powerful than our own sun. This might make our galaxy sound special, but it isn't. Scientists estimate that, with our present equipment, we can now see at least 15,000 million other galaxies similar to ours.

15,000 million galaxies, each with 15,000 million stars, each one of which is losing mass at around 4 million tonnes a second! What power, what magnificence, what majesty surrounds us! If all of this was created by God in an instant, how powerful must God be!

Put it another way. If our God has the power to create such a universe, then walking on water, or healing the sick, would not present him with a problem! Neither would raising his Son from the dead – in fact, it's just the sort of thing he might do to show who was boss around here!

Bible study notes — *Did Jesus rise from the dead?*

Read   Matthew 28:11-15

The story circulated by the guards was that Jesus did not rise from the dead but that his body was taken from the tomb in the night by his disciples. The disciples, on the other hand, claimed that Jesus did rise from the dead and that the High Priests bribed the guards to lie about what happened.

Which is the truth? Clearly, this is not just an academic question of interest only to historians, it's a question with far-reaching implications for everyone in the world! In short, the Resurrection is an essential part of the Christian faith. In fact, if Jesus did not rise from the dead, then the New Testament claim that he is the Son of God would have little to commend it! As St. Paul wrote in his letter to the church in Corinth, 'And if Christ has not been raised, our preaching is useless and so is your faith' (1 Corinthians 15:14). So what is the evidence for the Resurrection?

Jesus the carpenter   Jesus was born to a young peasant woman, in an isolated town, in a remote area of the Roman Empire. Even had he been born a Roman citizen, there is little he could have done to have risen from such obscurity to world-wide fame, but born into a Jewish family, living in an occupied land, and then growing up to work as a simple village carpenter . . . ?

So how can it be that two thousand years later

and half-way round the world, here you are, reading this book about the life and death of this man called Jesus? What other village carpenters do you know who lived and died in the Middle East, two thousand years ago? Or two hundred years ago? Or even twenty years ago?

On the face of it, Jesus was a simple man from humble beginnings who lived in an occupied land. He received no special schooling or education and, for the last three years of his life, he made himself homeless, travelling from town to town as an itinerant preacher. Finally, he was rejected by his own people and executed as a common criminal. How can it be that this man became the most famous person in history?

How convincing are the arguments that this can be explained simply in human terms, that Jesus was just an extraordinary man?

Dispirited disciples

When Jesus was taken away to be tried and executed, his disciples watched helplessly as their world collapsed around them. The joy of their triumphal entry into Jerusalem only days earlier, suddenly turned into the despair of men and women who had seen all their hopes and dreams destroyed at a stroke. The disciples had believed that Jesus was the Christ, the Messiah. They saw him not only as he their friend, their teacher, and their leader, but also as the future leader and redeemer of the Jewish nation. They had listened in awe to his teaching, they had been amazed at his miracles, they had even seen him raise the dead. And then, after they had come to believe that nothing could stop him, they had seen him taken away and put to death on a cross.

Suddenly they were alone, hiding from the

Roman soldiers and the Jewish authorities and not knowing what to do. Some of them began to set off back to their homes, hoping to pick up the lives they had left behind three years earlier. Then something happened to change those defeated, despairing and cowering men and women into the confident, outspoken and death-defying disciples who set about establishing a church which eventually spread throughout the whole world. What could have brought about this dramatic change in these people? Can this be explained in human terms?

Jesus the preacher Jesus began his ministry when he was about thirty years old, walking from town to town with his band of followers and preaching to the townspeople who came to hear him. He was not trained as a preacher and his education in the Jewish Scriptures (our Old Testament) was only that of any boy born to a Jewish family. After only three years as a preacher, at the age of thirty-three, he was executed.

After his death, stories about his preaching, his death and his resurrection began to spread throughout the world.

Supposing you suddenly discovered that you had only three years to live. What could you do over those next three years to ensure that, two thousand years later, people all over the world would know your name? You would have radio and television to help you, but even so, how could you possibly ensure that your name would continue to be topical thousands of years after your death?

Could it be that the name of Jesus continues to be topical through the centuries purely by chance, or is it because he is not dead, but is alive and active in his people throughout the world?

Martyred disciples

Immediately after Jesus was seized, the disciples were terrified of the Romans and of the chief priests. Peter, who had been so confident and self-assured while he was with Jesus, was so afraid that he denied even knowing Jesus. Later, after Jesus had been crucified, the disciples hid themselves away and were afraid to venture outside or even to open the door of their hide-out.

We do not know what befell all the disciples, but we do know that:

- Peter was crucified upside down.
- Andrew (Peter's brother) was crucified in Achaia (southern Greece).
- James was put to death by Herod Agrippa I in AD 44.
- Bartholomew was skinned alive and then crucified upside down in Armenia.
- Stephen was stoned to death.
- Thomas (Doubting Thomas) was also martyred, although we are not sure how.
- And it is believed that Paul was also executed, although this is not certain.

How is it that so many of those frightened disciples were later willing to face the most horrendous deaths just for refusing to deny their faith? If they had indeed stolen the body of Jesus from the tomb in the night, if the Resurrection was indeed just a hoax, would they really have been willing to die in the ways they did? Few people are willing to die for the truth, would anyone be willing to die the deaths of those early Christians, just for a hoax?

If Jesus didn't rise from the dead, if the disciples had lied about his resurrection, how can their willingness to die for him be explained? What do you think? Did Jesus really rise from the dead?

Prayer

Lord,
   medicine is advancing at a great rate,
   new cures and vaccinations
   are being developed
   every day.
And yet, Lord,
   not a single physician
   or doctor
   has managed to raise
   a patient
   from the dead.
Something you managed to do
   2,000 years ago.

It's not surprising that we question
   whether this really happened.
   But we forget that you are God,
   that you have power and knowledge
   beyond our mortal comprehension.
Power and knowledge that created the universe
   we live in,
   right down to the cells which form
   the building blocks of our bodies.

Surely Lord,
   if you are capable of this,
   you are capable of anything.

It is so easy
   and natural
   for us, as mere people,
   to try and place
   our mortal constraints upon you,

but please help us to realise
just how ridiculous this is
and that, as God,
you can do anything you wish,
including raising your Son,
Jesus Christ,
from the dead.

Amen.

Chapter 2
Stranger than fiction

<u>Introduction</u>   It's hard to believe, I know, but surrounding every one of us, twenty-four hours a day, there are the voices of people talking and laughing and singing, and we just can't hear them! It's an amazing truth that the very air around us is filled with the sounds they are making but, because of the nature of the human body, none of us can hear what they are saying. In fact, without outside help, we would have no means of knowing these people even exist.

You're probably wondering what I'm going on about. Perhaps a different time zone or a parallel universe? Perhaps even another dimension?

The truth is that our human senses only operate within a very narrow field, they are only capable of detecting and processing a very small percentage of what is actually happening around us. The human ear, for example, can't detect the sound from a high-pitched dog whistle, and the human eye can't see X-rays.

Believe it or not, those people's voices really do exist. In fact, sophisticated electronic equipment now exists which not only detects those voices, but also makes them audible to us. This may sound amazing to you, but this equipment is now inexpensive and readily available. If you don't believe me, just go to any electrical retailer and ask them to demonstrate a radio!

The point I am trying to make is that we can only ever be aware of the things happening around us that fall within the range of our senses. Messages in the form of radio waves surround us every minute of every day, but without a radio receiver, we would have no way of knowing. It's easy to convince ourselves that we know everything that's going on around us, but in truth, we don't. We can be sure there is much more to the world in which we live than we can see and hear of it! And whoever said, 'What you don't know, can't hurt you' has never walked into a glass door!

Death is one of the things we will never fully understand, not in this life anyway. For example, most people would regard the dividing line between life and death as being pretty distinct. They would claim that they can look at an animal or plant and pronounce it dead or alive with a fair degree of accuracy. Well, perhaps they can, but . . .

A few years ago, I planted some 'annuals' in a flower bed in our garden at home. Now, 'annuals' flower in the same year they are planted and then die, so it never occurred to me that, over the following years, these plants would take over the entire garden, which shows how much I know about gardening!

But that's exactly what happened. You see, the dead plants were left in the flower bed too long, so, in due course, their seeds were dispersed by the wind. The strange thing is, before those seeds were released, each seed was part of a dead plant. So, were the seeds dead too? No, definitely not! Were they alive? Well, not really, not until they were released by the plant and allowed to germinate.

A similar vagueness can exist with more complex organisms. Recently, scientists were amazed to find that bacteria found on an insect encased in amber was still alive, having lain dormant for millions of years. Was that bacteria dead? No, definitely not! Was it alive? Well, not in the sense that you or I would understand, not until it was rejuvenated, anyway.

I started this chapter on the subject of radio waves and somehow ended up writing about dead plants and dormant bacteria. What these all have in common is that they remind me how little we really understand about the world in which we live. Things are never as simple as they appear. Take Jesus, for example. When people crowded round to hear him preach, they saw just an ordinary man. Of course, his preaching was good; he could tell a good yarn and he usually put things in a way they could understand. And some of his miracles were incredible; healing the sick was commonplace! But, on the face of it, the Jesus they flocked to see was just an ordinary man. But, and here's the question, was he an ordinary man with God-given powers, or an extra-ordinary man created by God, or what? Who or what was Jesus?

Bible study notes   *Who was Jesus?*

Several different pictures of Jesus have been passed down to us through the centuries. We have:

- Jesus the new-born baby, lying in a manger in a stable in Bethlehem; Jesus, 'the Christ Child'.
- Jesus the loyal son, supporting his mother, and his brothers and sisters, following the death of Joseph; Jesus, 'the Carpenter'.
- Jesus the teacher and the miracle-worker; Jesus, 'the Son of God'.
- Jesus on the cross, fulfilling his Father's plan for him; Jesus, 'the Lamb of God'.

Who, exactly, was Jesus?

Read   Colossians 1:15-22

This passage is part of a letter written by Saint Paul to the church at Colosse. The letter was written some time between AD 54 and AD 62, shortly before Saint Paul's death, and in his letter, Paul writes of Jesus, 'He is the image of the invisible God, the firstborn over all creation. For him all things were created: things in heaven and on earth . . . all things were created by him and for him. . . . For God was pleased to have all his fullness dwell in him.'

What does all this mean? How does this description of Jesus compare with the pictures of Jesus we looked at earlier? How does it compare with what Jesus said about himself?

When we think of Jesus as 'the Christ Child', the baby in the manger, we think of Jesus as having been created by God in the womb of Mary. But, in his letter, Paul wrote that Jesus was the Creator of everything, that, '. . . all things were created by him and for him'. This would suggest that Jesus existed before he first appeared as a baby in Mary's womb, in fact, that he existed right from the very beginning of time.

The picture we have of Jesus, 'the Carpenter' is of Jesus, the real man, working hard with his hands following the death of Joseph, to provide for his family. Jesus, the man, was no wimp, and when Paul wrote, 'But now he (God) has reconciled you through Christ's physical body through death . . .' he was referring to a man thirty-three years old, a man who was fit and strong, and a man who was accustomed to working hard for his living.

We often think of Jesus as, 'the Son of God', but in our normal understanding of a father/son relationship, the father always exists before the son. Is this also the case with God and Jesus? Did God exist before Jesus, did God create Jesus? Paul's letter seems to state quite clearly that this is not the case: 'For by him all things were created . . . all things were created by him and for him.' So how can Jesus be 'the Son of God' and yet be the Creator of everything?

And we think of Jesus as 'the Lamb of God', the Jesus who accepted death on a cross as the fulfilment of God's mission for him, as Paul puts it, '. . . making peace through his blood, shed on the cross'. What sort of a man was this Jesus that he was willing to sacrifice his all in obedience to God? And this wasn't blind obedience. Jesus knew what was going to happen to him and he knew that to avoid all that suffering, all he needed to do was to leave Jerusalem!

Perhaps this question, 'Who was Jesus?' is best answered by Jesus himself.

Read   John 10:30

Jesus said, 'I and the Father are one.' This would suggest that the life-force in Jesus was God himself, in other words, that Jesus was God, come to Earth. What do you believe?

Read   Mark 8:27-30

Try to imagine the scene. Jesus and his disciples were making their way towards the villages around Caesarea Philippi. No doubt they were chatting as they walked, probably about recent events. Perhaps they talked about the miraculous feeding of four thousand people with just seven loaves of bread, or about the healing of the blind man at Bethsaida. Suddenly Jesus dropped into the conversation what must have seemed like quite a casual question, 'Who do people say I am?'

It is easy to imagine the disciples laughing as they answered him, 'Some say John the Baptist; others say Elijah; and still others, one of the prophets.' They would laugh because they saw all these suggestions as silly. They were relaxed and they were off-guard when Jesus voiced the second part of his question, 'But what about you, who do you say I am?'

The laughter would die down; they hadn't foreseen the sting in the tail of Jesus' question.

It had been easy to mock the suggestions of others, now they were faced with the self-same question. They had travelled with Jesus, they had seen his miracles, they had heard his extraordinary teaching, now they were being asked to explain it all.

After a long moment, Peter spoke up. Peter the brusque, burly, confident fisherman, for once, perhaps, speaking in hushed tones: 'You are the Christ.'

Ultimately, it does not matter what claims other people make about Jesus. Ultimately, only one thing truly matters, the answer you give when Jesus asks, 'Who do you say I am?'

Prayer

Lord Jesus,
   you say that you are the Son of God,
   but you also say that you are
   God as a man.
So which is it to be, Lord?
Are you the Son,
   born in a manger
   to the Virgin Mary?
Who worked as a carpenter
   until he was thirty years old,
   then spent three years preaching,
   finally being killed on a wooden cross?
Sacrificed so that our sins
   might be forgiven?

Or are you God?
An omnipotent and wonderful God
   who created all things
   and chose to come to earth as a man,
   and live amongst us?

It is so difficult for us
   to believe that you are both;
   Father and Son,
   God and Man.
Yet that is exactly who you are.
The Christ,
   Emmanuel,
   Jesus,
   Our Lord.

Help us to understand.

Amen.

Chapter 3
Think small

Introduction

Imagine yourself sprawling on a sun-lounger on a warm summer afternoon. The sun is beating down from a clear blue sky and the sounds of summer from the garden surround you. Bees scurry between the flowers, gathering their harvest of nectar. Woodpigeons coo contentedly from the top of the apple tree, its branches motionless in the still summer air. Amidst all of this, completely relaxed, you kick off your shoes and luxuriate in the soft caress of the grass between your toes.

Now imagine a beetle crawling through the grass, happily going about his business on this warm summer afternoon. Above his head, the grass closes like a canopy, shading him from the worst heat of the sun, but also limiting his view of the sky and of the world around him. With grim determination, he weaves his way through the grass, relentlessly pressing on towards his destination. He stops for a moment, his curiosity raised by a small silver coin, half buried in the soil. It means nothing to him and so he scurries on, time is pressing. A few metres further and he sees an enormous pink lump in the grass ahead of him. Cautiously, he makes his way forward, the hairs on his legs bristling in alarm. It's like nothing he's ever seen before!

In case you haven't guessed, our imaginary beetle has stumbled across your big toe in the grass. And as he examines your big toe, what do you think that tiny beetle would be able to understand of your world, of your life, of your power, from the little bit of you he can see? The answer, of course, is not very much!

Yet that beetle can see more of you than you can see of God. And that beetle is nearer to you in terms of his world, his life, and his power, than you are to God. So how can you hope to understand God from what you can see of him?

Now suppose you wanted to communicate with that beetle. Suppose you wanted to tell him something about yourself and about the world you live in, how could you do that? The plain truth is, you couldn't, well, not unless you could turn yourself into a beetle, that is! Even then he would have only a limited understanding of what you were trying to tell him, but at least you would be able to try.

Bible study notes   *Why did Jesus come to earth?*

The story of Noah and the Great Flood is a story of God's anger at the wickedness of mankind. It is now thought likely that the biblical account of the Great Flood was based on a real flood which occurred around four thousand years ago and geologists have recently found evidence that, around that time, the Black Sea was created when the Mediterranean Sea burst through and flooded the low-lying land of what is now the Black Sea basin. Based on fact or not, the story of Noah and the Great Flood serves to illustrate the enormous gulf that exists between God and mankind. God is so very perfect in every way, and we are so very human! The two are just incompatible!

There was another occasion when God became angry with his people.

Read   Numbers 21:4-9

On this occasion, the Israelites saw the error of their ways and turned back to God who relented and told Moses to lift up a bronze snake for the people to look at and be saved. This particular story was used by Jesus when he was teaching Nicodemus.

Read   John 3:14-18

Poor Nicodemus found it difficult to understand the teaching of Jesus, but we now know that when Jesus talked about himself being 'lifted up', just like 'Moses lifted up the snake in the desert', he was referring to the Crucifixion!

Verses 16 and 17 of this reading are many people's favourite Bible passage, and understandably so. But when Jesus said, 'For God so loved the world . . .' what did he mean by 'the world'? If we search the Bible for guidance on this, we find that we can confidently state that Jesus didn't mean 'the Earth'. Nor did he mean the plants and the animals. No, we can be quite sure that what he was really saying was, 'God so loved people . . .' And, of course, we are people, so we would be correct in saying, 'God so loved us that he gave his one and only Son, that whoever believes in him shall not perish but have eternal life.'

This is reiterated in John 5:24.

In this and the previous passage, Jesus seems to be saying that the only condition for eternal life is to believe in him! Could it really be as simple as that?

Read John 11:25-26

Well, he couldn't have put it any more clearly, could he? But what about saying sorry for the things we've done wrong in the past and what about avoiding sin and trying to lead a perfect life in future? Surely there must be conditions to this eternal life? What happens if you truly believe in Jesus but continue to lead a sinful life? Surely that would justify God's condemnation?

Read John 12:47

Wow! Could it be that this eternal life thing really is something for nothing, a free gift? Is it possible that something so wonderful, so priceless, could be given away without any strings attached? Could God really require only that we believe in Jesus to be forgiven all our sins and to be given entry to the kingdom of heaven? The answer to these questions is very definitely, YES! YES! YES!

So, why did God send Jesus to Earth? To tell us about himself and to bridge that enormous gulf that separates him from us, perfection from imperfection. And how does he do that? Through the power of love – his love for us. A love so boundless that God was willing to sacrifice his only Son for our sake. A love so overwhelming that our sins are as nothing in its presence. A love so powerful that we are loved just the way we are, warts and all.

Jesus died so that our sins could be forgiven and so that we could join him in heaven. Think about it! If only people who lead blameless lives are allowed into heaven, then no one will ever get there! Jesus would have died for nothing!

So Jesus takes away the sins of those who believe in him and promises them eternal life. Now that's what I call a gift worth having!

Prayer

Lord,
  you are so wonderful,
  so unblemished,
  so perfect in every way.

And yet we are so bad,
  so sinful,
  so imperfect in every way.

How can we ever hope to get close to you.
To bridge the gulf
  that lies between us.

We may try to be good Christians,
  to understand your wisdom,
  to carry out your will
  and be free from sin.

But we let you down,
  time,
  after time,
  after time.

We have no hope of attaining
  your level of perfection.

At the same time,
  you can never lower your standards.
You can never be anything
  less than perfect.
But, Lord,
  you crossed the great divide
  when you came to earth
  as a man.

When you decided to live
　in human form
　and face the everyday trials
　and temptations
　as one of your own people.

Through Jesus, you were able
　to communicate with us.
You were able to make a new covenant
　with us.
A new relationship.

And in return, all you ask
　is that we acknowledge
　you
　as Lord.

And we do, Lord.

Amen.

Chapter 4
Idiot-proof!

Introduction

It was the October of 1854. British, French and Turkish troops were defending the Black Sea port of Balaclava against massive Russian forces. It was the Crimean War, and the port of Balaclava was the main supply port for the alliance armies and, therefore, vital to the war effort.

On the 25th October, Lord Raglan, who had overall command of the British forces, was watching the battle from a vantage point on high ground. On the flank of the main battlefield was a small artillery post which had been captured from the British by the Russians a few days earlier. As Lord Raglan surveyed the battlefield, he noticed a small force of Russian troops, working on the captured guns. As he watched, he quickly realised that the guns were being dismantled and removed. He decided this had to be stopped, and that the best way of doing this was to send in a small brigade of cavalry.

In 1854 there were no field telephones or radio transmitters and orders were passed down the line of command using messengers, either on horseback or on foot. It was through such an 'aide-de-camp', as these messengers were called, that Lord Raglan sent his order to Lord Cardigan, who commanded a suitably positioned brigade of cavalry. This messenger was instructed to tell Lord Cardigan to, 'Charge the captured gun positions.'

We will never know who, exactly, was responsible for the mistake, but the order Lord

Cardigan received, or thought he'd received, was, 'Charge and capture the gun positions.'

The difference in the wording of the two messages was not great, but the difference in the meaning of the instructions was very considerable. The intended order, to, 'charge the captured gun positions,' was an instruction for the brigade of cavalry to charge a small force of Russian soldiers on the flank of the main battlefield. The received order, to, 'charge and capture the gun positions,' was an instruction for the small brigade of cavalry to charge the main Russian heavy artillery at the far end of the valley.

The consequences of this mistake were dire. The order, as received, sent a light brigade of cavalry into a full frontal attack on the Russian gun emplacements. Six hundred and seventy men on horseback, with nothing more than side arms and swords, charged down the valley, directly into the line of fire of the Russian heavy artillery, manned and defended by three thousand Russian troops. The British cavalry brigade was virtually annihilated in what has now become known as, 'the Charge of the Light Brigade'. This was the tragic unforeseen end to the lives of many brave men who were willing to follow orders regardless of the personal sacrifice demanded.

And what about the death of Jesus? Was that also the tragic and unforeseen end to the life of a brave man who was willing to follow orders regardless of the personal sacrifice demanded?

Bible study notes   *Why did Jesus have to die for us?*

Read   John 10:17-18

Jesus predicted his death many times to his disciples towards the end of his ministry and he made it clear that he accepted the suffering it would involve as part of his work here on Earth. He was determined that his life was not going to be taken from him, it was going to be given by him.

So, the crucifixion of Jesus was not a tragic end to the work of Jesus, nor was it an unforeseen act against the will and plan of God; it was a vital part of God's plan for his Son. But why? Why did Jesus have to be sacrificed?

To understand the reasoning behind this, we have to recognise that, for whatever reason, God chose to reveal himself to the world through the Jewish people. It is through their extensive writings, which included what we now call our Old Testament, that we get our first glimpses of God at work in his world and involved with his people. And it is through these writings that we discover the importance of sacrifice to the Jewish people of Jesus' time. They had come to believe that one of the most effective ways to communicate with God was through sacrifice. If they wanted to ask for God's forgiveness or to say sorry for something they had done wrong, or if they wanted to thank God for a good harvest or some other blessing, or if they just wanted to enjoy fellowship with God and with each other, they did it through sacrifice. And the requirements for those sacrifices were laid down in detail in their Scriptures, particularly in the book of Leviticus.

Read   Leviticus 4:27-35

'In this way the priest will make atonement for him for the sin he has committed, and he will be forgiven.' If we study the book of Leviticus, we find that the greater the sin and the greater the forgiveness required, the greater the sacrifice that was necessary. We also find that one of the limitations of the forgiveness bought through sacrifice was that only the specific sins referred to were forgiven. Other sins not confessed, or perhaps not known about, and any future sins, were not covered by the offering.

We also find that any sacrifice offered to God had to be a perfect specimen, without defect. In this way, an Israelite could not just bring his diseased and dying animals for sacrifice, they had to be the best from his herd or flock, the ones he would have preferred to have kept. The offering had to involve real cost on the part of the giver, if it were to be successful.

So what does this have to do with the death of Jesus? Well, God wanted people to understand the true value of his gift in Jesus and so he used terms with which the Jewish people would be familiar. You see, Jesus was the greatest sacrifice that would ever be made, that could ever be made. He was the Son of God and no greater offering could ever be made. In fact, so great was he as an offering for sacrifice that all sins were forgiven as the result of his death, not just the sins confessed to God, not just the sins we know about, not even just the sins of the past! The very first Christians, because they were Jews, could understand the relevance of Jesus as a sacrifice and they could see how all sins, even those of the future, could be forgiven as the result of a sacrifice so great, a sacrifice so perfect, as Jesus.

So is this forgiveness for everybody? No! It most certainly is not! Supposing you were out with a friend when it suddenly started to rain and your friend ran into a shop and bought a raincoat as a gift for you. Would that gift of a raincoat protect you from the rain if you refused to accept it? Of course not! And the gift of forgiveness which Jesus offers us is just the same as that raincoat, it can only protect us if we accept it!

Another way of looking at it is this. One of the features of a sacrifice in Old Testament times, as we have already seen, was that it had to involve a cost on the part of the one seeking forgiveness. The sacrifice of Jesus is no different in this respect and if Jesus is nothing to you, how can his sacrifice have any cost or meaning for you? Obviously, it can't! Jesus made it clear, right through his ministry, that anyone who believes in him will be forgiven. By the same token, he also made it clear that those who do not believe in him, for whom his sacrifice has neither value nor meaning, those people, one day, will face him as their judge.

Prayer

Lord Jesus,
 you mean so very much to us.
You are our shepherd and guide.
Our confidante and friend,
 our healer,
 teacher,
 and preacher.
But more than all this,
 you are our saviour.

You took upon your shoulders
 the sins of the world
 and offered yourself
 as a sacrifice
 so that you could send
 a clear and distinct message to us,
 that we are forgiven
 and offered entry
 to the kingdom of heaven.

Lord,
 we can never thank you
 for all that you did,
 all you continue to do for us.

But we can
 and do
 return the love
 you give us.
Thank you, Lord.

Amen.

Chapter 5
Who loves ya, baby?

Introduction

I'd like to tell you about Phil. Phil's a good friend of mine who has some of the most amazing gifts and abilities. For instance, he can tell funny stories like no one else I know. Let me give you an example.

A few years ago we hitched up our caravan, and my wife, our two children, our two dogs and I, set off to the Dales for our family holiday. It was early spring, and to our delight, some members of Stage II, the Christian youth group we run, decided to pack their tents and sleeping bags and follow us. The sun was shining from a clear blue sky as we left North Lincolnshire and headed for Phil's beloved Wensleydale, where he lives. All the signs were for a thoroughly enjoyable week.

But the Dales are not in North Lincolnshire and even before we arrived at the campsite it had started to rain. And boy, it really rained! Within a few hours, the hilltops around us were fringed with waterfalls, silver torrents cascading from the escarpments into the valley below. By the end of the first day, most of the rivers through the Dales had burst their banks and flooded the roads and fields in the valley bottoms. After two or three days without let-up, farmers were losing their battle to rescue sheep and lambs trapped by the rising flood-waters.

The members of Stage II were also casualties of the notorious Dales weather and they were feeling particularly miserable the morning Phil came to visit. Their tents had blown down in the night, and the morning had dawned on tired and drawn faces, wet and muddy clothes and sleeping bags, and treasured possessions like stereos and cameras in a very sorry state. With ankle-deep water covering the campsite, camping was no longer an option. Unfortunately, with the roads out of Wensleydale by then flooded and impassable, neither was going home.

And then Phil arrived, and even before we'd found somewhere for him to sit (no small task with fourteen people and two big dogs in our touring caravan) he'd started telling his jokes and stories to cheer everyone up. The members of Stage II warmed to him immediately, as I knew they would, listening enthralled to his tales and anecdotes. For hour after hour, despite the rain hammering on the caravan roof, the sun was shining in our little world. Even the sodden boots and dripping anoraks by the door, and the piles of wet and muddy clothes strewn everywhere, were forgotten. It was magical!

Something else special about Phil is his strength. In all fairness, he's over six feet seven inches tall and built to match, so you'd expect him to be quite strong. But he is by far the strongest man I know.

Once, when we were repairing a car together (something we did a lot of as teenagers, since our cars were old and our funds limited) we found ourselves with no winch to lift the engine out of the car. To my amazement, Phil just leaned over the front of the car, waggled the engine off its mountings, and lifted it bodily out of the engine bay. I still remember watching in disbelief as he carried it out of the garage, chest high.

That's my friend, Phil. Someone with an amazingly strong personality, and someone with incredible physical strength too. And yet, despite these great strengths, Phil has a weakness. A real weakness! Something he just can't resist. Something he just can't leave alone. Something he refuses to give up, regardless of the cost involved. Phil's weakness is the Yorkshire Dales.

You see, Phil works in Teesside, but he loves the Yorkshire Dales so much, he has made his home in Wensleydale. Over the years, the money he has spent on travelling to work every day amounts to a small fortune. And the hours he has spent behind the wheel of a car, at the beginning and end of his normal working day, have to be calculated to be believed. Believe it or not, over the last ten years alone, the hours he has spent driving his car between home and work add up to the equivalent of over three years in full-time employment.

So Phil, that man of incredible strengths, has a weakness. And it might surprise you to learn that God, our God of incredible strengths, has a weakness, too. Our all-powerful, almighty God, the Creator of the universe in all its vastness and majesty, the Lord of life who knows every animal, bird, fish, and insect that's ever lived, has a weakness. A real weakness! Something he just can't resist. Something he just can't leave alone. Something he refuses to give up, regardless of the cost involved!

What's God's weakness?

You! He can't resist you! He just can't leave you alone! And he refuses to give up on you, regardless of the cost involved! There may be five thousand million people on this earth, but no one is quite like you. To God, you are unique.

Bible study notes

Did Jesus really die for me?

When people first begin to think about the death of Jesus and about what it means, they often find it difficult to accept that his sacrifice was for them, personally. After all, he died nearly two thousand years ago, long, long before our generation was born! How could he have died for people who didn't exist, who wouldn't exist for thousands of years? With all the millions and millions of people who have ever lived, who will ever live, how could he have died for you or me, personally, or for anyone as an individual?

This is an important question! Unless we can understand that Jesus died for each and every one of us as individuals, we cannot hope to understand the very personal nature of the gift of forgiveness!

We each need to think and pray this through for ourselves, and I have found that my prayers for a greater understanding of my faith are sometimes answered with miraculous speed! My own prayers on this were answered along the following lines, and while I know we all need to find our own ways of understanding these difficult concepts, I offer to you the following train of thought in the hope that it might be helpful:

Jesus Christ didn't die for mankind, he died for people. He died for all people, everywhere. He died for all people, in all times. I am one of the people he died for! He died for me!

Read John 14:1-4

Jesus said, 'I am going to prepare a place for you. And if I go and prepare a place for you, I will come back and take you to be with me that you also may be where I am.' (Verse 3.) This is not a vague, abstract promise, waved generally in the direction of mankind. This is a very personal promise, made to us, as individuals.

Usually, when people first become Christians, they suddenly find a deeper understanding of the forgiveness which Jesus bought for all of his believers. They readily accept that the sins and failings of their fellow Christians are forgiven and that a place is prepared for them in the kingdom of heaven. But all too often, they find it much harder to believe that this same forgiveness, and this same welcome, are for them too!

Their thinking goes something like this:

'Jesus wants you to be one of his disciples and he died so that your sins might be forgiven. I can understand him doing this for you, you are a nice person – not perfect, I know, but then no one ever is – but I can understand him loving you, you are a nice person. What I can't understand is why he would want me as a disciple, why he would want to die for me! I know you think I'm quite nice, but I know what I am really like, inside! And he knows what I am really like, inside! How could he possibly want me to be one of his disciples?

Read   Romans 3:21-24

There is no difference between us, we have all sinned and we all fall short of the glory of God.

Read   John 6:32-40

Jesus said, '. . . whoever comes to me I will never drive away' (Verse 37).

Read John 10:27-30

Jesus said, 'My sheep listen to my voice; I know them and they know me. I give them eternal life, and they shall never perish; no one can snatch them out of my hand.'

How comforting, to know that it's God's will that none of us be lost!

Prayer

Who am I, God,
   that you care about me?
That you love me?

There have been millions of people
   living over thousands of years.
I am not particularly special
   in any way.
I really don't stand out in a crowd.

Yet you know
   every hair on my head
   and every thought
   that passes through my mind.

To you I am unique,
   I am special.
So special that you even have
   a soft spot for me.
A weakness.
You love me so much,
   you even died for me.

Well, God,
   while I may be your weakness,
   I'm pleased to say
   that you
   are my strength.

Amen.

Chapter 6
The chosen few

Introduction

Saul of Tarsus was a powerful and influential man. We know this because he was a Pharisee (a member of an elite order which was held in very high regard by the ordinary Jews of that time) and he was a member of the Sanhedrin (the name for the Jewish senate or 'council of elders'). In other words he was one of the 'Jewish Authorities'. He was also, officially, a Roman citizen, which added to his authority, permitted him certain privileges, and entitled him to special treatment by the occupying Roman forces. Yes, Saul was a powerful and influential man.

Although he was born in Cilicia, in the city of Tarsus (from which he was given the title, 'Saul of Tarsus'), he spent most of his early life in Jerusalem. He was born into a devoutly Jewish family and he was raised in the Jewish tradition, eventually attending a rabbinic school and studying under Gamaliel, a highly respected teacher of the Jewish law. Saul was also intelligent, with a sharp intellect. He spoke several languages fluently and there can be little doubt that, as a man, he commanded the highest respect from those around him.

So, Saul was a devout Jew who believed in the one true God of Israel. He also believed that the Jews were God's chosen race and that devout living and the study of the scriptures held the key to eternal life. We can be certain that he held those beliefs with the utmost conviction, he was not the sort of man who would have been easily swayed.

Although he studied under Gamaliel, Saul's attitude towards the Christians was very different from that of his teacher. When the first apostles were brought before the Jewish council, it was Gamaliel who argued that no action should be taken against them. His view was that if Jesus were not the Son of God, then nothing would come of Christianity anyway, and if Jesus were the Son of God, then action against the disciples would be action against God, himself. The result was that the apostles were set free with just a warning.

But Saul's attitude towards the Christians was ruthless. When Stephen was accused of blasphemy, it was Saul who witnessed his stoning and gave approval to his death, even though, under Roman law, the Jewish leaders had no authority for such an act. The truth is, Saul was furious with the Christians and regarded them as a major threat to the Jewish faith.

Since we know that Saul was a man of God, we can be sure that he was persecuting the Christians, not because he was evil, or for any personal gain, but because he believed it was what God wanted him to do. He saw it as his duty to stamp-out the Christians and he set about this task with enthusiasm and determination. And so, in AD 35, some two years after he'd watched and approved Stephen's stoning, Saul approached the High Priest. He wanted, and received, the High Priest's authority to ferret out the Christians in Damascus and to bring them back to Jerusalem as prisoners.

We can be sure that Saul knew a great deal about the life and work of Jesus. He would also have been aware of the evidence for the resurrection of Jesus. He had, for example, seen and heard the personal witness of many of the disciples. We also know that he heard the dying testimony of Stephen. And yet, on its own, all this evidence was not enough to bring Saul to belief. Something else was needed.

The story of Saul's conversion on the road to Damascus, when he was confronted by the risen Jesus, is well known (Acts 9:1-19), and the effect on Saul was dramatic and immediate. Over the years that followed, Paul, as he was renamed, devoted his life to spreading the gospel of Jesus and he wrote much of what we now know as the New Testament.

Clearly, Jesus chose Saul to become one of his disciples. It wasn't the evidence he'd seen and heard about Jesus which eventually made Saul into a Christian, it was an instantaneous change brought about by a deliberate act of God.

Saul already believed in God before his conversion, but that wasn't and isn't enough for God – indeed, many of the religions of the world believe in the one true God. But what God wanted from him, and still wants from us, is that we accept Jesus as our Saviour, that we are Christians. In Saul's case, he was chosen to come to this belief by Jesus himself, but what about us? What brings us to this belief?

Bible study notes

How do we become disciples?

The story of Saul is powerful evidence for the resurrection of Jesus, and Paul wrote about his conversion in his letter to the churches in Galatia:

Read Galatians 1:11-24

It's strange, but true, that no amount of evidence is ever sufficient on its own to persuade someone to become a Christian. Something else is always needed. Paul was confronted by the risen Jesus on the road to Damascus, so he was clearly chosen by God to become a disciple. But what about us, how do we become disciples?

Read John 16:5-15

'But when he, the Spirit of truth, comes, he will guide you into all truth' (Verse 13).

So if evidence alone never produces a believer, what is this 'something else' which is needed? The answer is, the 'Spirit of truth' referred to in this passage from the gospel of John. This is just another name for the Holy Spirit, or the Spirit of God, which comes to us to open our eyes to the truth, to his truth! And when we receive the Holy Spirit, things that once seemed foolish, suddenly start to make sense! Teachings that once seemed strange and obscure, suddenly become easier to understand!

Read 1 Peter 2:9-10

Could it be that the disciples of Jesus really are 'a chosen people'?

Read John 15:16

As Jesus, himself, put it, 'You did not choose me, but I chose you!'

Search your heart. Can you believe? If you can, how does it feel to know that Jesus chose you, personally, to be one of his followers, to be a disciple? How does it feel, that just like Saul, or Paul as he later became known, God has chosen to reveal the truth of his Son to you! This is no small privilege! As Jesus himself said, 'For many are invited, but few are chosen' (Matthew 22:14).

Prayer

It's difficult sometimes, Lord,
   to believe in something we cannot see.
Someone we cannot hear.
We read the evidence
   suggesting that you exist,
   that you once lived on earth;
   God in man's image.

We hear that you were crucified on a cross,
   and then rose from the dead.

But in a scientific society,
   where we depend so much
   on what we can witness
   with our own senses,
   third-hand accounts
   just simply aren't enough.

Sometimes though, Lord,
   we do witness, at first-hand,
   the power of your Holy Spirit.
When we see you working in our lives,
   feel you touching us and holding us close,
   hear you speaking through our minds.

When this happens, Lord,
   we thank you that you have chosen
   to touch us in this way.
Chosen us to become Christians.

We ask you to help us
   to believe in you
   and come to know you
   as our Lord and Saviour.

Amen.

Chapter 7
The town drunk

Introduction

I met Durrell in Romania. We were delivering relief supplies and agricultural equipment to the people of Sintana and he arrived to help us unload the tractor. He was a lovely man, smiling and friendly, open and honest, and I warmed to him immediately.

You can imagine my surprise, then, on being told that eighteen months earlier he had been despised by everyone who knew him, which was just about everyone in the town Sintana! At that time, he was the Town Drunk, so it wasn't surprising that the townsfolk looked down their noses at him. But what they really loathed him for was the way he treated his family.

In the agricultural areas of Romania there is very little employment and even less in the way of money, and none of either for the Town Drunk. But Durrell's wife had managed to find a part-time job so she could feed their two children. Unfortunately, much of the money she earned was taken from her by Durrell, who was always desperate for money to buy drink. Then, when the money he had taken from her was spent, he returned home to beat her, convinced that she had yet more money which she had hidden from him.

Durrell's wife and children also suffered because of the way the other people in the town treated them. They were branded as 'Durrell's wife' and 'Durrell's kids' and most people would have nothing to do with them. Strangely, despite all the hardship and suffering, Durrell's wife and children loved him dearly.

One Sunday, Durrell's daughter attended the little Christian chapel in Sintana and found the people there friendly and welcoming. This was such a pleasant experience for her, she persuaded her mother and brother to go with her the following week. Again the people were pleased to see them and made them feel wanted. During the whole of the next week, Durrell's daughter worked on her father to persuade him to go with them to the chapel the following Sunday. Finally, Durrell agreed.

Durrell arrived at the chapel, more than a little apprehensive. It was one thing for the people there to welcome the Town Drunk's family, quite another for them to welcome the man himself! And yet, despite his fears, he was made welcome, and not in just a formal, reserved manner, but with a genuine, warm affection.

The two services I attended in that little chapel were simple but filled with the joy of worship and the warmth of Christian love. After one of those services, I witnessed half the congregation going to the front of the chapel in order to make a commitment to Christ. Probably something similar happened at that first service Durrell attended. However it came about, Durrell asked Jesus to come into his life at that very first service he attended and his whole world was changed. I am pleased to be able to tell you that, as I write this, nearly five years later, he has never touched alcohol since. It's an amazing truth that the man who used to beat his wife for money and leave his children to go hungry, is now the chapel treasurer, trusted with all the church's funds.

No one in that chapel would claim any credit for the miraculous change which occurred in Durrell that day, they rightly put it down to the work of the Holy Spirit. But the warm Christian love they showed first to Durrell's daughter and finally to Durrell himself, enabled the Holy Spirit to work in their little chapel and to save that wonderful man whom I am proud to call my brother.

Perhaps we should all reflect on how we would react if our 'Town Drunk' appeared in the church doorway one Sunday morning.

Bible study notes   *What does Jesus ask from us?*

Before we consider the question of what Jesus is asking from us, we need to understand, right from the outset, that we cannot earn our way into the kingdom of heaven. No matter how hard we try to lead a blameless life, no matter what good deeds we do, no matter how perfect we try to be, God's forgiveness and his promise of eternal life are available to us for one reason and one reason only – they are a gift from God through Jesus.

And that gift is available to everyone who holds firm to the belief that Jesus is the Son of God. Strange as it may seem to us at first, providing we hold firm to that belief, our subsequent behaviour does not affect this gift, although it must often sadden and greatly hurt our loving, wonderful, heavenly Father. As I have said already, but it's certainly worth repeating, if only Christians who lead blameless lives were admitted to the kingdom of heaven, Christ would have died for nothing! So when we look at what Jesus asks of us, we must remember that these are not conditions for eternal life, we are not expected to be perfect (although we are asked to try!) and, by the same token, neither should we expect other Christians to be perfect!

Read   Matthew 19:16-26

Jesus told the rich young man that if he wanted to have eternal life, he must keep the commandments. Although the young man replied that he already did this, Jesus looked into the young man's heart and saw the problem. The young man worshipped his wealth and, as Jesus taught, you can't worship two gods. The rich young man was not living by faith in God, but by faith in his wealth. The disciples were amazed at Jesus' comment that it is easier for a camel to go through the eye of a needle than for a rich man to enter the kingdom of God. They were amazed because, in the Jewish society of that time, it was believed that rich men were rich because they were blessed by God! Fortunately, Jesus went on to reassure his disciples that all things are possible for God, and no doubt he had in mind the purpose of the cross that awaited him!

(Incidentally, they do say that it is easier for a camel to go through the eye of a needle if you put it in a liquidiser first!)

Read Matthew 22:34-40

What does Jesus ask of us? To keep the commandments, yes, but especially:

- to love the Lord our God with all our heart and with all our soul and with all our mind.
- to love our neighbour as ourself.

The first of these 'special' commandments follows on from Jesus' teaching that we can't worship two gods. If we love the Lord our God with all our heart and with all our soul and with all our mind, any other 'personal god' we might have is very definitely pushed into second place. The second of these two commandments can also be pretty demanding!

Read   Luke 15:11-32

The parable of the Prodigal Son begins with the statement that there was a man who had two sons, so Jesus clearly intended, right from the start, that this story was to be more than just a simple illustration of the love and forgiveness of God, wonderful as that is! Had this been his only purpose, only the wayward son would have been needed in the story. So why did Jesus include the older, loyal, son? What else was Jesus wanting us to think about?

If the younger son in this parable represents the repentant sinner being welcomed back by God, perhaps the older son represents the committed church member (or youth group member!) working hard and turning out week after week only to feel put-out when a lot of fuss is made over someone new. Clearly, we should all be aware that this requirement to love our neighbour demands not just fine words but a sustained, continuous, and practical response that extends well beyond the boundaries we would choose to set! There can be no doubt that the response of those people in that little chapel in Sintana when Durrell suddenly appeared in the doorway, was exactly what Jesus wanted from his 'elder son' and exactly what we should be aiming for.

Prayer

Lord,
    you made us as one family,
    brothers and sisters,
    living together in your name.
And Lord,
    you asked us to love each other,
    to care for each other,
    to help each other
    in a way
    that the members of any family should.

But so often we fail
    to carry out your will, Lord.
So often we are unkind,
    selfish and thoughtless.
We live in a world
    where hate, prejudice
    and snobbery are rife.

So Lord,
    help us to stand apart
    from the ways of this world.
Help us to show love for one another,
    so that people may see your love
    shining through us.

Amen.

Chapter 8
The gift

Introduction

It was cold and bleak, spring comes late to the Transylvania Mountains and the wind still had a vicious bite to it. The village was nothing more than a collection of shacks built on the side of the mountain and huddled together as if seeking shelter from the wind. Most looked barely strong enough to survive the all too frequent mountain storms, but one shack was worse than the rest. It had only a small earth yard, dug from the hillside, and it was broken and dilapidated. It was also tiny, with just one room in which all the family lived and slept. John and Aurel exchanged glances, they'd been searching for Cornel's home for some time, and what they'd found shocked them.

I first met Cornel the previous November, at the home of Aurel, the pastor of the little chapel in Sintana. Later that day, Cornel borrowed a guitar on which he played the hymns for the service in the chapel and later still, at the home of one of the church elders, he accompanied the choir as they sang Romanian Christmas carols to us. It was a wonderful evening and we were amazed at Cornel's incredible skill as a guitarist. He wasn't just accomplished, he was gifted, which was all the more remarkable because Cornel didn't possess a guitar of his own, and because he had a terribly deformed right hand.

Gordon Gatward, a Methodist Minister and one of the drivers on that trip, learned from Cornel that his dream was to play a Yamaha acoustic guitar. So, once he was back in England, Gordon set about raising the money to buy him one and, in due course, a new Yamaha guitar was dispatched with the Reverend John Fenner on his next trip to Romania. Strangely, by the time John arrived in Sintana with the guitar, Cornel was no longer attending its little chapel and no one had seen or heard from him for some time. John and Aurel set about finding him, which proved difficult, but at last they knocked on the door of his home, wondering what they would find inside.

Cornel was pleased to see them, but he was also embarrassed, ashamed of the poverty of his home with its bare floor and meagre furnishings. He was also ashamed that his young wife and baby were having to live in such conditions, but he was out of work and no one would hire him. Why should they? Why should they employ a man with only one good hand when there were countless able-bodied men seeking work?

Cornel and his wife were destitute. Their only source of income was a small plastic bowl fitted with an electric light bulb. Cornel's wife used this to incubate hens' eggs given to her by their neighbours. The success rate wasn't good, but selling the few chicks that hatched brought in a little money for food. In fairness, because of his deformity, Cornel had been offered a disability allowance, but it was only two pounds per month and to claim it he was required to sign that he would never work again. He'd refused, he wanted to work, it was just that nobody wanted him!

Cornel invited John and Aurel into his home and asked them to sit on the bed; there were no chairs. They placed the cardboard box in front of him and asked him to open it. He looked at it, uncertain what to do, for some reason afraid of what he might find.

'Open it!' they encouraged, and finally he did, finding inside the new Yamaha guitar. He remembered his conversation with Gordon and thought they had brought it for him just to try, something he had said was his dream. How could he explain to them? How could he tell them, that was yesterday's dream, now meaningless? His only dream now was to support his family!

'It's yours!' they said, 'a gift,' and he stared at them in disbelief. It couldn't be true! Did they realise what they were giving him? Not just a guitar! Not just the means of playing carols at Christmas and hymns at church services. What they were giving him was a means of supporting his family! He could earn his living playing a guitar like that! He could play at weddings, christenings, parties and even village fetes! Even his deformed hand wouldn't matter, it didn't prevent him playing the guitar, so it wouldn't stop him supporting his family! After a long moment he picked up the guitar and slowly held it up to the light to admire it. A tear rolled down his cheek, he could hardly bring himself to speak, he just didn't know what to say.

John and Aurel could see that things were desperate for Cornel and his family. The guitar held promise for the future, but their immediate needs were urgent. So, there and then, Cornel was offered the post of Musical Director at the chapel in Sintana. It wouldn't pay a huge wage, but enough to enable him to feed his family and get back on his feet. The chapel would have music again, and Cornel would have his dignity and hope.

Christian love has to be more than just compassion and concern, it requires action where action is needed. That gift of a guitar had been intended as just a small act of kindness, but in the hands of God . . .

Bible study notes

What does it mean, to love our neighbour?

Read Luke 10:25-37

Jesus used the parable of the Good Samaritan to illustrate how he wants us to love one another. In this parable, the Samaritan helped the injured man, not because he was obliged to, but because he cared about him. And it is not enough for us just to pay lip-service to this requirement that we love one another. The love we are asked to show each other must be genuine and, when necessary, practical, which often means there will be a cost to bear.

How easy it is for us to be diverted from our responsibility towards each other. If the children of the family next door were dying from lack of food, we would need little encouragement to do something about it. But when the house they live in isn't next door but in a foreign land, and when we only see their swollen stomachs and drawn faces on television, we are much slower to provide the help they need! Our neighbours are world-wide and we ought to remember that the children of foreign lands are just as important to God as the children living next door; Jesus died for them just as much as he died for us!

Another point to note about the illustration which Jesus used, is that the Good Samaritan went far beyond what we might regard as sufficient. He not only helped the injured man and took him to an inn, he also told the innkeeper he would meet all the costs from his own pocket. This is an example which Jesus wants us to follow. He does not want us to love our neighbours grudgingly, doing only just enough to enable them to get by, he wants us to love our neighbours generously, to give to them and to help them, without counting the cost! In fact, he wants us to love our neighbours the way he loved us, which means, without any limits! He even told us this later in his ministry:

Read   John 15:12

If his instruction to love our neighbours as we love ourselves was difficult to follow, how much harder is this later command?

Read   James 2:14-26

When Jesus died on the cross, he died for everyone! He gave his life for the alcoholic who beats his wife just as much as he did for the nun living in a convent. And if Jesus was willing to die for the hungry and the homeless of the world, how can we claim to be followers of Jesus and yet turn our backs on them?

Prayer

Lord,
    they call it Compassion Fatigue.
The new social disease
    which is eating away
    at the hearts and minds
    of everyday people.

It is this disease which allows us
    to sit by and watch
    scenes of devastation and suffering
    on television
    without even flinching,
    never mind actually doing something
    constructive to help.

Lord God,
    when you called us to be Christians
    and intructed us to love our neighbours,
    you didn't just mean
    Vera and Bob next door
    who we happen to like.
You meant all people,
    whether or not we like them,
    whether or not we even know them.

And loving people
    doesn't just mean
    not harming them
    or wishing them well.

It means actively seizing
    every opportunity we have
    to practically demonstrate
    our love,
    and the love of God.

Help us to realise this, Lord.

Amen.

Chapter 9
Surprise! Surprise!

Introduction The British luxury liner *Titanic* was a beautiful ship. She had a displacement of 66,000 tonnes, a length of eight hundred and eighty-two feet (about 269 metres) and a cruising speed of twenty-four knots, fast even by modern standards. The *Titanic* was also of an entirely new design, and had been proclaimed unsinkable because of her sixteen watertight compartments. On the 10th April 1912, she set sail on her maiden voyage from Southampton to New York City.

Considerable publicity had surrounded the building and launching of the *Titanic* and the number of people wanting to sail on her far exceeded the number of berths available. Those who secured reservations were understandably proud to be on such a beautiful ship for her maiden voyage. One of the consequences of this was that there was incredible demand from passengers on the *Titanic* wanting to send messages to their friends and families over the ship-to-shore radio. In addition, many of the passengers on the *Titanic* were wealthy businessmen, with their own reasons for wanting to send and receive messages.

The result was that the radio operator on board the *Titanic* found himself under enormous pressure. So much so, that several messages which he intercepted from other ships in the area, warning of unusually heavy pack-ice, were never passed to the bridge. At 11 pm on the 14th April 1912, the United States Ship *Californian* radioed the *Titanic* to warn her that the ice was so heavy and thick that she, herself, had been forced to stop. The officers of the *Californian* knew that the *Titanic* was sailing directly towards them, and directly into the same thick pack-ice.

Once again, the warning was not passed on to the ship's officers on the bridge and at one time it was reported that the radio operator aboard the *Titanic* sent the following message in reply, 'Shut up, shut up, I'm busy!'

Only forty minutes later, with her navigation lights within sight of the *Californian*, the *Titanic* collided with an iceberg, ninety-five miles south of the Grand Banks of Newfoundland and without having reduced speed at all.

The iceberg punctured five of the sixteen watertight compartments of the *Titanic*, one more than had been considered possible when she was designed, and the stricken ship sank in less than three hours with the loss of over 1,500 passengers and crew. The *Californian*, so very close, failed to come to her rescue because her radio operator was off duty and asleep.

So many warnings, all of which were ignored. And so it was with Jesus! So many warnings, there in the Scriptures, and yet the Jewish Authorities, who prided themselves on their knowledge of the scriptures, failed to see the signs.

Bible study notes

What was written in the Scriptures concerning Jesus?

At the time of Jesus, the 'Scriptures' were what we now refer to as the 'Old Testament'. So what was written in the Scriptures concerning Jesus? Well, for the most part, we will need to limit our brief look at the Old Testament, to the book of Isaiah.

Read Isaiah 7:13-14

'The virgin will be with child and will give birth to a son, and will call him Immanuel.' (It should also be noted that the meaning of the Hebrew name, Immanuel, is 'God with us'.)

Read Isaiah 9:1-7

It is hard to believe that these two passages were written over 700 years before Jesus was born (especially verses 6 to 7, 'For unto us a child is born . . . and he will be called Wonderful Counsellor, Mighty God, Everlasting Father, Prince of Peace.'). In verse 7, Isaiah prophesies, 'He will reign on David's throne and over his kingdom, establishing it and upholding it with justice and righteousness from that time on and for ever.' If we try to interpret this prophecy in human terms, it is clearly an impossibility, human kings cannot reign for ever! So how could this everlasting kingdom be established? The last part of verse 7 tell us, 'The zeal of the Lord Almighty will accomplish this.' Humanly speaking, it was impossible but, for God, of course, nothing is impossible, and his plans were already in place.

Read   Isaiah 11:1-5 and 12:1-6

In this passage, Isaiah starts his prophecy with the words, 'A shoot will come up from the stump of Jesse.' Now Jesse was the father of King David, so Isaiah was promising that this 'Holy One of Israel' would be of King David's line, which is consistent with his earlier prophecies that this new King would reign on David's throne for ever. And the meaning of Isaiah's prophecy that the Lord would become our salvation (12:2) certainly will not be lost on Christians!

Read   Isaiah 35:5-10

In this passage, Isaiah prophesied that the blind would see, the deaf would hear, and the lame would walk, a prophecy only fulfilled in Jesus. He also said that there would be a highway called 'the Way of Holiness' and it is interesting that the early Christian church adopted the name 'the Way', perhaps from its use in this passage (for an example see Acts 9:2). Isaiah also speaks of the 'redeemed' and the 'ransomed of the Lord' (verses 9 and 10), phrases now frequently used to describe Christians.

Read   Isaiah 42:1-7

Again, there is much in this passage which Christians can interpret as prophecies concerning Jesus, but there is one particular prophecy which is especially important. It is to be found in verse 6, 'I, the Lord . . . will make you to be a covenant for the people and a light for the Gentiles.' There is little in the Old Testament which suggests that the God of the Jews is also concerned with the well-being of the Gentiles; by and large the Jews regarded themselves as the 'chosen race', God's favoured people. However, Jesus made it clear that he came to Earth for all people, not just for the Jews, and this is exactly what this passage from the book of Isaiah can be interpreted as saying.

All of the texts that we have looked at so far have come from the book of Isaiah, but there is one final passage I would like you to read which is to be found in the book of Psalms. It is the passage from which Jesus himself quoted as he hung on the cross. He said, 'My God, my God, why have you forsaken me?' (see Matthew 27:46). What was he trying to tell us? Was he trying to say that in those final moments he felt genuinely forsaken by God (and had, therefore, experienced all aspects of what it means to be human)? Or was he referring us to Psalm 22, so that we might have some insight into what was prophesied for him and some understanding of what he was suffering for our sake?

Read Psalm 22 and try to imagine what it was like for Jesus as he hung on that cross.

Prayer

Lord,
  it's so easy to get bogged down
  in everyday life.
Rushing around,
  too busy to either pray or take time out
  to 'listen' to God.
And it's so easy to read the scriptures
  without seeing what lies before our very eyes,
  without ever truly understanding
  what has been written.
We criticise the early Jews
  for failing to see who Jesus was,
  yet so often we are guilty
  of doing exactly the same thing.

And so, Lord,
  we really must ask ourselves,
  if you were to return
  to earth tomorrow,
  would we be ready?
Would we understand?
Would we know who you are?

Or would we ignore the evidence
  that lies at our own finger tips.

Lord, help us to hear
  when you call,
  to heed all the warnings,
  so we will never be guilty
  of denying you.

Amen.

Chapter 10
Truly amazing!

Introduction   Imagine that we made a model of the earth, the size of a tennis ball, and placed it at the foot of Big Ben, in the centre of London. On that scale, where would we place our model of the sun? On the other side of the Thames? On the outskirts of London? In Cornwall? No, believe it or not, somewhere around Gibraltar, off the southern tip of Spain! And how big would our model of the sun need to be? The size of a football? The size of a weather balloon? The size of a hot air balloon? No, a ball five miles in diameter!

The farthest (known) planet from the sun in our solar system is Pluto, a small, desolate lump of rock, believed to be coated with methane ice. Our model of Pluto would need to be about the size of a child's small marble, but where would we place our marble? The answer is, about 30,000 miles away, or around a seventh of the way to the moon.

So, even with earth reduced to the size of a tennis ball, our solar system is still pretty big. But what about the other stars in our galaxy; where in our scale model would we place the star which is our nearest neighbour? Well, stars in the Alpha Centauri group are the nearest stars to earth, and in our scale model they would have to be placed about 150 million miles away. Wow, that's a long way away!

In that case, what about the farthest known object in the universe, where would that be in our scale model? The answer is about 900,000 million, million miles away – and that's at a scale where the earth is reduced to the size of a tennis ball!

The speeds found in our universe can be similarly mind-blowing. On earth, most people would regard a car driven at a hundred miles per hour as fast, especially if they were being followed by a police car! Of course, aeroplanes can travel at much higher speeds than this, but even *Concorde* seems slow when compared with interstellar speeds.

For example, while you are reading this book you are travelling at over a thousand miles per hour as a result of the Earth spinning on its axis once a day.

But you are also travelling through space at over 67,000 miles per hour as a result of the earth going round the sun once a year.

Even that enormous speed is slow compared to the speed with which our galaxy rotates around its centre. Incredibly, our solar system travels around the centre of our galaxy at around 620,000 miles per hour.

But all the galaxies in the universe are also travelling away from each other, and the speed of our galaxy (and the speed of you, reading this book!) relative to the farthest galaxies, is of the order of 600 million miles per hour!

Examining the universe in this way is a wonderful means of gaining an insight into the power of God who created it all; it certainly reminds us that his power is way beyond our understanding. But no matter how much scientists learn about our universe, or how long we gaze in wonder at the marvels of creation, we will never find concrete evidence that it was all the work of God. That will always have to be a matter of faith.

Bible study notes   *What does it mean, to live by faith?*

How would you describe what is meant by 'faith'? Most people would probably describe 'faith' as something like, 'believing, despite the absence of proof'.

God could easily provide us with proof that Jesus was his Son, this would be a simple matter for him, and then there would be no need for us to have faith. However, for most of us, God chooses not to provide this proof, so we must assume that God wants us to be free to respond to his Spirit and to believe, or not believe, as we choose. Clearly, God regards our faith as important, he doesn't want followers who have had their minds made up for them!

Read   Hebrews 10:35-39

In this letter to the Hebrews, we find, 'But my righteous one will live by faith, and if he shrinks back, I will not be pleased with him' (Verse 38). So, our faith is important to God, and he calls upon us to 'live by faith'. But what does it mean, to live by faith?

Read   Hebrews 11:1

Here we have a more demanding definition of 'faith', being sure of what we hope for and certain of what we do not see. So to live by faith, under this definition, would mean to live as if we had no doubts at all that Jesus is the Son of God.

And if we really did have this degree of certainty in Jesus, surely our whole outlook on life would be different. Wouldn't we then be much more ready to accept that this life is just temporary and that the real life is the one to come? Wouldn't we be much more willing to sacrifice our hopes and ambitions for this life, on the basis that our primary purpose is to follow Jesus? In other words, wouldn't we be much more willing to live to please God, rather than ourselves?

Read　Jude 17-23

This 'Call to Persevere' by Jude, was written by him to encourage disciples to live by faith. He tells us to, 'Keep yourselves in God's love as you wait for the mercy of our Lord Jesus Christ to bring you eternal life' (Verse 21). In other words, we must live our lives in the way Jesus would want us to (i.e. keeping ourselves in God's love) while continuing to hold fast to our belief in Jesus Christ with his promise of mercy and eternal life.
　　So how do we go about, 'living by faith'?

Read　Hebrews 12:1-3

In this brief passage from the letter to the Hebrews, we are called to live by faith, with the encouragement, '. . . let us run with perseverance the race marked out for us.' The letter then continues with a suggestion as to how we should set about this task. It proposes, 'Let us fix our eyes on Jesus . . .'

Read John 15:9-17

If we fix our eyes on Jesus, we find one particular command which is repeated over and over again, that we should love each other. It's funny how we keep coming back to this instruction, isn't it? You might even be forgiven for thinking it's my own particular obsession! However, it was Jesus who wanted to emphasise this particular instruction to us, and if we wish to live by faith, this instruction has to come high up our 'list of things to do'.

Read Hebrews 4:14-16

This short passage has a simple but vital message for us all. Hold firmly to your faith, believe in Jesus, and you will receive mercy and eternal life. And this is the truth, because Jesus is for *you*!

Prayer

Lord,
we have so much in this life
to worry and think about,
so many reasons to be anxious,
so many things to doubt.

But you call us to live by faith,
to place our trust in you,
and live according to your will.

This isn't always easy, Lord.
If it was, then everyone would do it.
But the extra effort is certainly worth it.
Because, by saying that we believe in you,
not only are we given
access to your kingdom,
but by realising your presence in our lives,
we are suddenly aware of guidance,
love,
and an inner peace
that has always been offered to us,
but, until now,
we had not even been aware of.

So now, as you call us
to have faith in you,
we know that what you ask of us
is a great deal,
but we also know
that what you have given in return,
is far greater.

And for this, Lord,
we are forever thankful.

Amen.